If the World Were a Village

A Book about the World's People

If the World Were a Village

A Book about the World's People

Written by David J. Smith

Illustrated by Shelagh Armstrong

Kids Can Press

Acknowledgments

The effort, help and faith of many people were required for this book to be published. Jill Kneerim and Paulette Kaufmann both saw the value of it as long ago as 1992. I've had invaluable help from Barbara Bruce Williams, my agent. Val Wyatt, my editor, worked tirelessly through 14 manuscripts, never giving up hope that we would find the right combinations. And Pat Wolfe deserves special mention for everything she did. But most of all, this book is for Suzanne, my sunshine and my *bella luna*, who never stopped believing.

A note on numbers and dates

The term "billion" means different things in different parts of the world. In this book, it means one thousand million, or 1 000 000 000.

Calendars often refer to dates before the year 1 as B.C., or before Christ, and dates after the year 1 as A.D., or anno Domini, a Latin term meaning "in the year of the Lord." However, most people in the world prefer to use the terms B.C.E., or before the common era, and C.E., or of the common era. For this book about the global village, B.C.E. and C.E. have been used.

Text © 2002 David J. Smith
Illustrations © 2002 Shelagh Armstrong

Information updated July 2007

Kids Can Press acknowledges the financial support of the Ontario Arts Council, the Canada Council for the Arts and the Government of Canada, through the BPIDP, for our publishing activity.

Published in Canada by
Kids Can Press Ltd.
29 Birch Avenue
Toronto, ON M4V 1E2

Published in the U.S. by
Kids Can Press Ltd.
2250 Military Road
Tonawanda, NY 14150

www.kidscanpress.com

The artwork in this book was rendered in acrylic. The text is set in Bodoni.

Edited by Valerie Wyatt
Designed by Marie Bartholomew

Printed and bound in China

This book is smyth sewn casebound.

CM 02 20 19 18 17 16 15

National Library of Canada Cataloguing in Publication Data

Smith, David J. (David Julian), 1944–
  If the world were a village : a book about the world's people

Includes bibliographical references.
ISBN 978-1-55074-779-9

  1. Population — Juvenile literature.
2. Human geography — Juvenile literature.
I. Armstrong, Shelagh, 1961– II. Title.

HB883.S6 2002   j304.6   C2001-901749-9

Kids Can Press is a Corus™ Entertainment company

Contents

Welcome to the global village

Earth is a crowded place, and it is getting more crowded all the time. As of July 1, 2007, the world's population was 6 billion, 600 million — that's 6 600 000 000. Twenty-four countries have more than 50 million (50 000 000) people. Eleven countries each have more than 100 million (100 000 000) people. China has over 1 billion, 300 million (1 300 000 000), while India has over 1 billion, 100 million (1 100 000 000) people.

Numbers this big are hard to understand, but what if we imagined the whole population of the world as a village of just 100 people? In this imaginary village, each person would represent more than 66 million (66 000 000) people from the real world.

One hundred people would fit nicely into a small village. By learning about the villagers — who they are and how they live — perhaps we can find out more about our neighbors in the real world and the problems our planet may face in the future.

Ready to enter the global village? Go down into the valley and walk through the gates. Dawn is chasing away the night shadows. The smell of wood smoke hangs in the air. A baby awakes and cries.

Come and meet the people of the global village.

Nationalities

The village stirs and comes to life, ready for a new day. Who are the people of the global village? Where do they come from?

Of the 100 people in the global village:

61 are from Asia
14 are from Africa
11 are from Europe
 8 are from South America, Central America (including Mexico) and the Caribbean
 5 are from Canada and the United States
 1 is from Oceania (an area that includes Australia, New Zealand and the islands of the south, west and central Pacific)

More than half the people in the global village come from the 6 most populated countries:

20 are from China
17 are from India
 5 are from the United States
 4 are from Indonesia
 3 are from Brazil
 3 are from Pakistan

Languages

"Ni hao ma?" "Hello!" "Namaste!" "Zdraz-vooy-teh." "¡Hola!" "Ahlan." "Selamat pagi." The villagers greet one another in a babel of tongues. What languages do the people of the global village speak?

In the global village there are almost 6000 languages, but more than half of the people speak these 8 languages:

21   speak a Chinese dialect — of these people, 16 speak the Mandarin dialect
 9   speak English
 9   speak Hindi
 7   speak Spanish
 4   speak Arabic
 4   speak Bengali
 3   speak Portuguese
 3   speak Russian

If you could say hello in these 8 languages, you could greet well over half the people in the village.

Ages

A ball flies by and the children cheer.
There are many children in the village.
One-fifth of the villagers are 9 years of
age or under. More than half are under
30. Here are the ages of the villagers:

9   are children under age 5

9   are children between 5 and 9

18   are between 10 and 19

17   are between 20 and 29

15   are between 30 and 39

12   are between 40 and 49

9   are between 50 and 59

6   are between 60 and 69

4   are between 70 and 79

1   is over 79

On average, 1 person dies and 3
babies are born every year. A baby
born in the village today can
expect to live to age 63.

Religions

A bell chimes in a church, a wooden gong sounds at a temple, a muezzin leads prayers from the minaret of a mosque. The villagers are called to worship.

What religions do the people of the village follow? In the village of 100 people:

32   are Christians
20   are Muslims
14   are Hindus
 9   practice shamanism, animism and other folk religions
 6   are Buddhists
 2   belong to other global religions, such as the Baha'i faith, Confucianism, Shintoism, Sikhism or Jainism
 1   is Jewish
16   are non-religious

Food

The smells and sounds of the market draw you near. The tables are piled with fresh baked bread, vegetables, tofu and rice. Chickens cluck and ducks quack. In a pen not far away, a cow moos at the passing crowd.

The villagers have many animals. They help to produce food or are a source of food. There are:

- 31 sheep and goats
- 23 cows, bulls and oxen
- 15 pigs
- 3 camels
- 2 horses
- 250 chickens — yes, there are more than twice as many chickens as people in the global village!

There is no shortage of food in the global village. If all the food were divided equally, everyone would have enough to eat. But the food isn't divided equally. So although there is enough to feed the villagers, not everyone is well fed:

- 50 people do not have a reliable source of food and are hungry some or all of the time.
- 20 other people are severely undernourished.

Only 30 people always have enough to eat.

Air and water

In most of the village, the air is healthy and the water is clean. But not all villagers are so fortunate. For some, the air and water are soured by pollution, putting them at risk for diseases. Or water may be in short supply. Instead of turning on a tap, some villagers must walk long distances to find clean water.

Fresh air and drinkable water are necessities. How many people in the village of 100 have clean air and a nearby source of clean water?

83 have access to a source of safe water either in their homes or within a short distance. The other 17 do not and must spend a large part of each day simply getting safe water. Most of the work of collecting water is done by women and girls.

57 have access to adequate sanitation — they have public or household sewage disposal — while 43 do not.

68 breathe clean air, while 32 breathe air that is unhealthy because of pollution.

18

Schooling and literacy

A school bell calls the young people of the village to school. But for some children, there is no school to go to, or they must work instead, to help feed their family.

How many people in the village of 100 go to school?

There are 36 school-aged villagers (ages 5 to 24), but only 30 of them attend school. There is 1 teacher for these students.

Not everybody in the global village is encouraged to learn to read, write and think. Of the 73 people over age 15, 64 can read at least a little, but 17 cannot read at all. More males are taught to read than females.

Money and possessions

In one part of the village, someone buys a new car. In another, a man repairs the family's bicycle, their most valued possession.

How much money do people in the global village have?

If all the money in the village were divided equally, each person would have about $9350 US dollars per year. But in the global village, money isn't divided equally.

The richest 10 people have over half the money. Each has more than $25 000 a year.

The poorest 10 people each have only about $1 a day.

The other 80 people have something in between. Seventy-five of the 100 people in the village average about $4 a day.

The average cost of food, shelter and other necessities in the village is about $5000 per year. Many people don't have enough money to meet these basic needs.

24.

Electricity

Dusk arrives, then darkness. In many homes, electric light spills out into the streets. In others, the dark is kept away with candles, oil lamps and lanterns.

How many people in the village of 100 have electricity?

76 have electricity
24 do not

Of the 76 who have electricity, most use it only for light at night. In the global village, light is the one basic necessity that electricity provides. But some villagers have other luxuries that depend on electricity. In the village there are:

42 radios
28 televisions (7 with cable)
61 telephones (over 40 of these are cell phones)
15 computers

1000 B.C.E.

500 B.C.E.

1 C.E.

1650

1500

1800

1900

26

1000

2007

The village in the past

Today, 100 people live in the global village. How many people lived here in the past?

Over 3000 years, the population of the global village doubled 5 times, from 1 person to 2 people, to 4, to 8, to 16, to 32.

Around 1000 B.C.E., only 1 person lived in the village.

In 500 B.C.E., 2 people lived in the village.

In 1 C.E., 3 people lived in the village.

In 1000, 5 people lived in the village.

In 1500, 8 people lived in the village.

In 1650, 10 people lived in the village.

In 1800, 17 people lived in the village.

In 1900, 32 people lived in the village.

In 2007, 100 people live in the village.

The village in the future

What will our village be like in the future? How fast will it grow? How many people will it be home to?

Today, the village of 100 is growing at a rate of about 1.2 people a year. If there are 100 people in the year 2007, there will be more than 101 in 2008 and so on.

By the year 2100 or sooner, there will be 200 people in the village, and the number will reach 250 by 2150 or so. This is an important number, because many experts think that 250 is the maximum number of people the village can sustain. And even then, there may be widespread shortages of food, shelter and other resources.

Fortunately, groups such as the United Nations and many governments and private organizations are working hard to make sure that the village of the future is a good home for all who live in it. Their goal is a global village in which food, shelter and other necessities are basic rights for all.

Teaching children about the global village

This book is about "world-mindedness," which is an attitude, an approach to life. It is the sense that our planet is actually a village, and we share this small, precious village with our neighbors. Knowing who our neighbors are, where they live and how they live, will help us live in peace.

How can parents, teachers and group leaders foster world-mindedness in children? My experience teaching and leading workshops with children all over the world has taught me a few things. Here are some guidelines and examples of activities you might want to try.

• Make sure children have a map of the world in their heads. A strong sense of world geography lays a foundation for discussions with or about people of other regions, countries and cultures.

Have a good, up-to-date world map prominently displayed on a wall. Refer to it to locate places in the news, countries where friends or relatives are traveling, areas where the books you are reading take place, and so on. Also, if possible, have at least one atlas with a good index, so that you and your children will be able to find places and explore the world more easily.

Play geography games while on car trips, at meals, before class — anytime there is a lull. For example, try "What's next," a game in which one person names two contiguous countries, provinces or states, and the other people have to figure out what the next contiguous place is. For example, if I said "Canada, United States," you'd say "Mexico" because if I went from Canada to the United States, the next country on my trip would be Mexico. If I said "India, Nepal," you'd say "China"; if I said "Liberia, Ivory Coast," you'd say "Ghana."

"Capital/Country" is another good game. One person names a capital or a country and the other players must name the missing capital or country. For example, if I said "Lithuania," you would have to name the capital, Vilnius. If I said "Astana," you'd have to name the country, Kazakhstan.

Or play "Details," in which one person names a country and the other players have to give details about it. For example, for Italy, the details might be: capital is Rome; language is Italian; borders France, Switzerland, Austria and Slovenia; east is the Adriatic Sea, west is the Tyrrhenian Sea and south are the Ionian and Mediterranean Seas; entirely contained within it are the countries of San Marino and Vatican City.

Most importantly, ask questions all the time: Where is that? Where do they live? What language do they speak? What's it like there?

• Connect learning with doing. While knowledge of the world map is a vital first step, it is critical to get children doing things with people in other countries and cultures. This can be done in person or at a distance, through regular or electronic mail, Web activities and global teleconferencing.

Many Web sites have been constructed purely for this purpose. You'll find links to these sites through the large index and gateway sites, such as Yahoo! (http://www.yahoo.com), or check our global village Web site (http://www.mapping.com/gv) for updated data and links.

If you don't have access to the World Wide Web, or don't want to use it, try networking. See if you can prove "six degrees of separation": Ask a child to get a letter to someone in, say, Israel by sending the letter to somebody who may know somebody in that part of the world. Is it possible to get the letter to its destination via only six people? Be sure to ask the recipient to write back to explain how the letter reached him or her.

Have your child's school or homeschool association partner with a similar school or group in another country.

If your community is "sistered" with a community elsewhere in the world, get some information from your local government about the paired community and write to it.

• Help children learn to identify what they don't know. When studying the world and its people, think in terms of *possible* answers, not just *right* answers. Think also of open questions to which no answers are known. Discussion of such questions is a wonderful way to teach children how citizens think. Here are some sample questions to get you started:

If there's really enough food in the world, why do some people still go hungry?

What is a country? Why are there so many new ones trying for autonomy?

Why do so many people want to live somewhere else? Where are people migrating?

What forms of government do different countries have? Why are there so many forms of government? What are the advantages and disadvantages of each? You can get specific information about forms of government from several sources. Many of these sources are listed on page 32.

What do you think could be done to help the world's population growth rate slow down?

• Foster world-minded thoughts: Look out for your neighbor. Do not break faith with anybody in the community. Service is an important part of what citizens do. Being on a team is very important.

There are no secret formulas or activities here, just one truth: If we model the behavior, our children will follow our lead.

• Encourage passion. Do whatever is necessary to help children become passionate about their world, to discover their passions and build on and with them, and to learn from and about them. The people who are going to solve world crises 30 years from now are today's children. We'll be very, very lucky indeed if they are in a home or classroom where they acquire a passion for travel and landscape and exploration and culture and reading.

Children learn about passion from seeing it in action. What are you passionate about? How can you include children in the activities you are passionate about?

Make sure children see your love of maps and travel, your interest in news from other parts of the world and your curiosity about other people, cultures and languages. They may not follow your particular passion, but they will learn what it means to care deeply about something. If children express a strong interest in something, help them follow up and learn more.

In a way, all the opportunities for global connections through e-mail and television make the dream of a unified world look more achievable today than it did in the past. But in other ways, the making-it-come-true part is harder than ever, especially when you consider that the global dream includes adequate food and housing for all, universal literacy, the elimination of unhealthy water supplies and abundant, safe and affordable energy supplies. These goals will only be realized if we can find a way to stabilize the world's population. June 16, 1999, was Six Billion Day, and we continue to grow by 100 million people per year.

Understanding geography, the Earth and the people who live here — where, why and how — is a good starting point. However, what we need is not just facts, but a way of looking at the world that tells the story truthfully. We need to become truly world-minded and to foster that attitude in our children.

David J. Smith

A note on sources and how the calculations were made

As of 2007, there are 6.6 billion (6 600 000 000) people in the world, so in our village of 100, each person represents more than 66 million (66 000 000). Any time a fractional person would have appeared in our village, it was rounded to the nearest whole number.

Many different books and resources were used to collect data. The statistics were often surprising, especially because not all of the sources agreed.

While there is general agreement from one source to another on most of the statistics used in this book, there is some variation from year to year and source to source. The most notable area of disagreement was in predictions for future population growth, but there were also disagreements about food supply, education and clean air and water.

Whenever possible, the most current statistics have been used; if necessary, averages or extrapolations have been made from related information.

The following sources were used for the first edition of this book. The data were adjusted in 2007 using the most recent statistics available.

Report WP/91 to WP/98, *World Population Profile: 1991 to 1998*. U.S. Census Bureau. Washington, D.C.: U.S. Government Printing Office, 1991–1998 (http://www. census.gov/ipc).

State of the World: A Worldwatch Institute Report on Progress toward a Sustainable Society. Linda Starke, ed. New York: W.W. Norton & Co., 1994–2006 (http://www.worldwatch.org).

The Central Intelligence Agency World Factbook. Washington, D.C.: Government Printing Office, 1992–2006 (http://www.odci.gov/cia/ publications/factbook).

The Information Please Almanac. Otto Johnson, ed. Boston: Houghton Mifflin, 1996–1998 (http://www.infoplease.com).

The New York Times Almanac. John W. Wright, ed. New York: Penguin Putnam, 1997–2006.

The State of the World's Children. Carol Bellamy, ed. New York: United Nations Publications, 2000, 2004, 2006 (http://www.unicef.org).

The Time Almanac. Borgna Brunner, ed. Boston: Information Please LLC, 1999–2006.

The United Nations Human Development Report. United Nations Development Programme. New York: United Nations Publications, 1992–2006 (http://www.un.org).

The Universal Almanac. John W. Wright, ed. New York: Andrews & McMeel, 1992–1996.

The World Almanac and Book of Facts. Robert Famighetti, ed. New Jersey: World Almanac Books, 1996–2006.

The World Development Report. World Bank. New York: Oxford University Press, 1992–2006 (http://www.worldbank.org).

World Resources: A Report by the World Resources Institute in collaboration with the United Nations Environment Programme and the United Nations Development Programme. New York: Oxford University Press, 1992–1993 to 1998–1999 (http://www.wri.org).

Vital Signs, The Environmental Trends That Are Shaping Our Future. Worldwatch Institute. Linda Starke, ed. New York: W.W. Norton & Co., 1992–2006 (http://www.worldwatch.org).

I also used many pamphlets and printouts from the UN Food and Agriculture Organization and other UN agencies, found through the UN Web site (http://www.un.org) and the U.S. Census Bureau Web site (http://www.census.gov).

The following books and atlases also provided data:

The Economist Pocket World in Figures. The Economist. London: Profile Books, 1996.

The Economist World Atlas. The Economist. London: Profile Books, 1996.

Goode's World Atlas. Edward B. Espenshade, Jr., ed. Chicago: Rand McNally, 1998. (This atlas is particularly useful because it has a wonderful section of thematic maps.)

Kurian, George T. *The New Book of World Rankings*. Chicago: Fitzroy Dearborn Publishers, 1994, p. 32.

McEvedy, Colin, and Richard Jones. *The Atlas of World Population History*. New York: Penguin Books, 1978.

The National Geographic Atlas of the World. Washington, D.C.: National Geographic Society, 1995.

The National Geographic Satellite Atlas of the World. Washington, D.C.: National Geographic Society, 1998.